Original title:
Echoes in the Evergreen

Copyright © 2025 Creative Arts Management OÜ
All rights reserved.

Author: Kieran Blackwood
ISBN HARDBACK: 978-1-80567-243-2
ISBN PAPERBACK: 978-1-80567-542-6

Odes to the Forgotten Forest

In the woods where the squirrels play,
Lost shoes seem to dance and sway.
A raccoon wears a shiny hat,
Claiming he's the king—imagine that!

Trees gossip with the breeze at night,
Whispering secrets, oh what a sight!
One tree says, "I used to be grand,"
While the others just laugh, "Take a stand!"

Mushrooms sprout, throwing a bash,
Inviting all, even the old trash.
A paper cup brings the punch all night,
While the raccoon twirls in pure delight.

The owl, wise and slightly aloof,
Watches the party from the roof.
"Whoo!" he hoots, his laughter rings,
As the bushes dance, and the forest sings.

Callings from the Quiet Grove

In the hush of the trees, a squirrel shouts loud,
As he scolds the breeze, drawing quite a crowd.
A chorus of rustles, a laugh lost in flight,
It's nature's own joke, in the soft morning light.

Birds chirp a tune that sounds slightly off-key,
While a raccoon winks, like he's part of the spree.
Leaves tumble down with a giggling sway,
And the forest just chuckles, in its quirky way.

Reflections on the Forest Floor

Mushrooms in hats are having a ball,
Hosting a dance, where the critters all crawl.
A beetle with taps, and a snail on a groove,
Nature's odd band in a rhythmic move.

Pine cones are falling like awkward confetti,
Each thud a reminder that life's never petty.
A deer does a twist as the fox prances near,
While the trees all applaud with a rustling cheer.

The Enchantment of Winding Trails

Winding paths tumble, like a clumsy old coot,
Where roots love to trip you, and laughter's the loot.
A frog sings a ditty, it may not be sweet,
But you can't help but join in on the day's silly beat.

The shadows play tricks, making faces with glee,
As the leaves whisper secrets to old Mr. Tree.
With each misstep, a giggle escapes,
Chasing down sunlight, in all of its shapes.

Chords of the Crumbling Bark

Old trunks collect stories, with grooves like a smile,
Playing tunes of the past, for a while and a mile.
A woodpecker hammers, with rhythm and flair,
He's a rock star in nature, with no time to spare.

Branches sway gently, like dancers at play,
Each twist a reminder, to laugh all the way.
As clouds float above, with a chuckle or two,
The forest stands proud, in its whimsical hue.

Verses in the Canopy's Embrace

Up high the squirrels make a mess,
Chasing dreams in acorn dress.
With each leap they zig and zag,
While birds above just laugh and brag.

The branches stretch, they start to bend,
As raccoons plot to steal a friend.
The wise old owl keeps rolling eyes,
At all the chaos and the lies.

Sighs of the Ageless Timber

The trees stand tall, they really creak,
With secrets told by rugged beak.
Beneath the shade, the ants parade,
In tiny hats, they serenade.

A beetle dons a flashy tie,
While ladybugs just zoom on by.
They giggle soft with little quirks,
In this green realm, where nature works.

Humming in the Heart of the Forest

A chipmunk sings a silly tune,
While rabbits dance underneath the moon.
The trees are swaying, keeping beat,
As nature's band brings tasty treats.

In mossy shoes, they tap and twirl,
Each twist and shout, a joyful whirl.
The fireflies join in with glee,
Creating sparks for all to see.

Tales Written in Bark and Blossom

The bark tells tales of seasons past,
From winter's chill to summer's blast.
With every ring, a joke it spins,
Of squirrel wins and cheeky sins.

The flowers giggle in bright hues,
With petals rustling playful news.
They sway and dance without a care,
While whispers linger in the air.

The Language of Rustling Fronds

In the forest, whispers play,
Leaves giggle in the sway.
Branches swing with a wink,
Nature's chat as we think.

Squirrels gossip, oh so spry,
Telling tales as birds fly by.
Mossy jokes make trees snicker,
In this place, the laughs grow thicker.

Vows Written in the Roots

Beneath the ground, in secret pacts,
Roots swap stories, strange little facts.
They promise to share the rain and sun,
A partnership that's just good fun.

Worms hold conferences in the dirt,
Discussing what to wear, or flirt.
Critters chuckle at the tree stump's jest,
With roots that twine, they're truly blessed.

Gleams of Sunlit Serenity

Sunshine winks through the green leaves,
　Tickling the shy flowers that please.
Bees hum hymns while butterflies dance,
　Even the toadstools join in the prance.

A lazy breeze brings giggles aloft,
　Nature's humor, tender and soft.
Each beam sparkles with playful mirth,
In this bright world, there's endless worth.

Threads of Life Intertwined

Vines twist and turn with a chuckle,
Making friends in a friendly huddle.
Ferns wave high, wearing their best,
They know how to have a little jest.

Bark claps hands with roots below,
Sharing secrets of the ebb and flow.
In this twilit glen of trees so grand,
The jests of life are simply unplanned.

Reveries in the Verdant Shade

In the forest, a squirrel jokes,
Flipping acorns, cracking folks.
Trees chuckle when branches bend,
Who knew nature could pretend?

Ants march on in silly lines,
Arguing over food and wines.
A rabbit hops, a dance to see,
While deer roll eyes, just let it be!

The owls hoot with wise old grins,
As raccoons plot mischievous wins.
Underneath the leafy bow,
Nature's comedy on show!

So if you find yourself out here,
Just listen close, lend an ear.
Laughter rustles in the breeze,
Life's a joke among the trees!

Chants of the Emerald Sanctuary

Underneath the canopy's fold,
A parrot sings, a tale retold.
Frogs croak rhythms, offbeat tunes,
While drumming bugs dance with the moons!

The fox joins in with a wagging tail,
His stunts would surely never fail.
A bear snorts, then starts to sway,
As if to join this grand ballet!

Branches sway to nature's beat,
A concert that can't be discreet.
Even the rocks tap their feet,
Nature's rhythm, oh so sweet!

From dusk till dawn, they all unite,
In a symphony of pure delight.
Each laugh a note, each rustle a song,
In this forest where we all belong!

The Soundtrack of the Silva

Crickets strum on tiny strings,
Breeze hums softly, oh what it brings!
Bees buzz harmonies so sweet,
Nature band plays, can't take a seat!

Mice join in with a squeaky cheer,
As the wind whistles, lending an ear.
The brook babbles clever rhymes,
While stones giggle at passing times!

Trees sway gently, their laughter loud,
A symphony, proud and not cowed.
Each critter lends a unique sound,
A concert of joy, all around!

So tune in close, let rhythm flow,
Nature has an amusing show.
In every leaf and bark, there lies,
A melody under the skies!

Aspirations in the Arbor's Embrace

Beneath the branches, dreams take flight,
A raccoon dreams of disco night.
Squirrels plotting a comedy act,
With nutty punchlines that are packed!

A woodpecker taps out a joke,
While chatty bluejays add a poke.
The sun beams down, a happy face,
As critters gather, find their place!

Each blossom wears a goofy grin,
While rabbits debate who'll win the spin.
Nature's playground, playful and free,
A family of laughs, just wait and see!

So join the fun, take a seat,
In this wild world, favorites you'll meet.
For laughter blooms in every space,
In this grand, green, splendid place!

The Chorus of Forgotten Paths

Lost between roots and rocks,
Squirrels giggle at their socks.
Trees lean close to hear the fuss,
As raccoons plot in secret plus.

A rabbit sings the silliest tune,
Under the light of a bright full moon.
Bushes sway with laughter clear,
While owls hoot, 'What brings you here?'

The wind joins in, a quirky choir,
Tickling leaves, a prancing flyer.
In the woods where fun's at play,
Each path hums its own ballet.

So wander off the beaten track,
Where mischief wears a leafy backpack.
Among the giggles, let thoughts unfurl,
In this jolly, green-spun world.

Murmurs of the Leafy Haven

In a glade where shadows dance,
Frogs in tuxedos take their chance.
With tiny hats and monocles too,
They croak sweet tunes, just for you.

Butterflies waltz, a colorful sight,
Twirling in circles, a pure delight.
The sun joins in, a dazzling guide,
While hedgehogs swing to the rise and tide.

A bear with shades, lounging proud,
Cheers the antics of the crowd.
Laughter woven in every leaf,
In this haven, there's no grief.

So tiptoe softly, join the fun,
As the day fades into one.
In this leafy, joyful nest,
Share a chuckle, and feel blessed.

Notes from the Nature's Heart

The brook hums soft, a serenade,
As fish do flips, a splash parade.
Bamboo stalks sway, like a band,
Playing songs from Nature's hand.

A wily fox with a wink and grin,
Draws a map for a daring spin.
"Here's where the beetles gather round,
For a gala, last heard sound!"

Grasshoppers tap their tiny feet,
Joining the rhythm, oh so sweet.
Even the ants, in lines so neat,
Groove in unison, can't be beat.

So take a note from trees so wise,
Sing out loud beneath the skies.
In the heart of spaces green and bright,
Life's a party, day and night.

The Wisdom of the Whispering Trees

Among the branches, secrets brew,
With tales of many a critter crew.
Acorns drop with a thud and crack,
While branches sway, never slack.

A wise old owl spins yarns so sweet,
Of disco parties at woodsy feet.
Raccoons in tuxes, doing the twist,
With cheeky grins that can't be missed.

Squirrels trade their nutty jokes,
As laughter rings, and fun provokes.
The trees lean closer, ears perked high,
"Do share your tales, oh my, oh my!"

So gather 'round where whispers flow,
In a world where merriment grows.
For in the woods, life's never dreary,
Just laugh along; it's all quite cheery.

Shadows Among the Conifers

Shadows skip like playful sprites,
Chasing squirrels and birds in flights.
A tree trunk tells a funny joke,
As laughter rolls, the branches poke.

Beneath a bough, a raccoon sneezes,
Leaves flutter down like thousand breezes.
A sprightly fox plays hide and seek,
While critters giggle, oh so sleek.

Pinecones fall, with a thud, they land,
As the wise old owl gives a wave of his hand.
"Let's have a dance, oh trees so tall!"
They sway and twist, nature's grand ball.

In this green world, the fun won't cease,
Each gust of wind brings a bit of mischief.
The shadows laugh, a jolly band,
Among the conifers, so unplanned.

The Sound of Ancient Leaves

Rustles whisper secrets light,
Leaves chuckle softly, what a sight!
Nature's comedians, they flutter and sway,
With gossip that brightens up the day.

A leaf that tickles a spunky beetle,
Says, "Let's go play, I'll be your steeple!"
Mossy rocks join in with a grin,
"No stone left unturned, let the games begin!"

Old branches creak with ancient flair,
As squirrels debate on the best style to wear.
"Those acorns look so very chic!"
Each fashion critic from tree to peak.

The sun peeks in, a curious friend,
Watching the antics never seems to end.
In this leafy realm, so lively and bright,
Laughter rings out, what a delightful sight.

Timeless Voices in the Thicket

In the thicket, secrets bloom,
Whispers rise, dispelling gloom.
"Did you hear? The fern just snorted!"
The laughter echoes, and all are escorted.

Bushes gossip with a festive air,
While ladybugs dance without a care.
"Let's throw a party beneath the sun!"
A gathering of leaves, oh what fun!

Old twigs bark laughter, in playful jest,
Raccoons and rabbits strut their best.
"Tree to tree, let's trade some tales,
Of wild adventures and daring fails!"

Timeless voices, nature's cheer,
Bringing joy, and friends so near.
In this thicket, merriment reigns,
With jubilant stories that never wane.

Murmurs Beneath the Canopy

Beneath the canopy, giggles abound,
With furtive whispers, a raucous sound.
"Did you see that jumpy hare?"
"Not as high as my lofty flair!"

The groundhog sings with a croaky tune,
While bees rave about the bright afternoon.
"Buzz along, let's have some fun!"
In this green realm, all races run.

The mushrooms giggle, hats all aglow,
Encouraging bunnies to put on a show.
"Let's tap dance on that old damp log!"
They prance around, what a lively dialogue!

Under the leaves, the laughter swells,
As nature weaves its merry spells.
Murmurs of joy, and smiles that gleam,
In this forest, life's a happy dream.

Songs from the Bursting Buds

A chorus of frogs in a leafy parade,
Singing loud tunes that they happily played.
The squirrels all danced with their acorn hats,
While the old trees chuckled at all of that.

When blossoms burst forth like confetti in May,
The branches all laughed, what a bright, silly day!
With petals like hats on their leafy old crowns,
They twirl with the breezes, never with frowns.

Each bee buzzes goofy, on nectar they snack,
A floral buffet, no thought of a back!
Trees whisper secrets, the funniest tease,
Of the squirrels' mischief and bumblebees' sneeze.

A lighthearted breeze gives a tickle to bark,
As the shadows attempt a tree-mimic park.
Laughter cascades from the branches up high,
In a quirky old grove where the giggles won't die.

The Embrace of the Ancient Boughs

In a tree's great hug, all the critters convene,
Be it legless lizard or squeaky raccoon.
Their whispers of wisdom are coated in fun,
A comfy old hug from the root to the sun.

A wise owl spins tales about feathered flops,
While chipmunks debate which way is "top tops."
The squirrels keep racing, with acorns in tow,
Who knew that high branches could bring such a show?

Branches shake hands with wobbly old vines,
Rooted in laughter, their hardened designs.
With plenty of quirks, it's a sight to behold,
A cozy camaraderie, timeless and bold.

Yet in this great hug, all the ruckus is sweet,
The woodpecker's knock is a rhythm to beat.
With each joyful rustle, nature's pure scheme,
Sings laughter and smiles, like a glorious dream.

Myths of the Heartwood

In the heart of the woods, stories come to life,
Of mischievous fairies with a penchant for strife.
They sprinkle some laughter on branches so grand,
While the squirrels debate on who started the band.

A chipmunk once thought himself wise as a sage,
Debating life's troubles from his verdant stage.
His buddies would giggle, would tell all the tales,
Of his quest for enlightenment, a pile of snails!

The owls ask questions that are silly and stark,
"Who won the last match between trees and a lark?"
While the ferns chuckle softly at moss-covered stone,
And the lichen just sighs, "Can I please be alone?"

By the heartwood's age, the fun never ends,
With stories of beams and the laughter of friends.
Nature's own theater, where all can perform,
And the punchlines of life make the forest a charm.

Fluttering Dreams in the Glen

Amidst the bright glen, butterflies prance,
In colors so bold, they invite you to dance.
As the grass giggles softly, feeling the breeze,
The flowers all sway, like they're doing a tease.

Dreams flutter by on the wings of a bug,
While the sun casts a gaze, quite warm and snug.
The daisies debate if they're daisies or dreams,
In this whimsical world where nothing is what it seems.

With whispers of laughter, the trees join the jest,
As the sunbeam parade claims a sparkling quest.
Each petal's a smile in this playful ballet,
Where the shadows play tag with the light of the day.

So come join the party in this glen full of cheer,
Where nature's giggles ring out loud and clear.
Fluttering dreams make a whimsical scene,
In the heart of the glen, forever serene.

Voices Beneath the Endless Sky

Amidst the trees, the squirrels chatter,
Their nutty tales grow fatter and fatter.
A hawk takes a dive, but oh what a miss,
It swoops for a snack, but gets just a kiss!

The rabbits giggle as they play tag,
With every leap, they punch and brag.
A hare in the race trips over a vine,
And rolls down the hill, what a grand design!

Beneath the clouds, the cows moo loud,
While frogs in the pond gather a crowd.
A goat on a ledge strikes a pose so grand,
But slips on a rock, oh isn't life planned?

As shadows grow long, the sun starts to fade,
The critters retreat to their leafy glade.
With laughter behind as the day bids adieu,
The woods close their eyes, who knows what's anew?

The Harmony of Nature's Breath

In the morning light, the crickets tease,
While busy bees hustle 'round the trees.
A wise old owl pretends to be sage,
But hoots out a joke, it's quite the outrage!

The rustling leaves play hide and seek,
As the deer practice their best ballet technique.
A chipmunk joins in, with flair on the side,
But slips in the dirt—what a wild ride!

Beneath the branches, laughter does swell,
As mischievous raccoons ring a dinner bell.
They dine on the fruit—what a glorious buffet,
But trip on a peach, oh what a display!

As dusk settles down, the field mice convene,
With secretive whispers, conspiratorial gleam.
Their plans for the night, delightfully wacky,
As shadows dance in the dark, oh so tacky!

Chants of the Woodland Beings

High above, the owls profess their flair,
While wisecracking crows drop truths everywhere.
An antlered deer shares tales of the day,
But falls on a branch—oh what dire play!

The frogs in the pond have their nightly croon,
Hoping to catch a nice thunderous tune.
A fish leaps up, just aiming for fun,
But lands in a patch where two turtles run!

From bushes arise the bunnies' next feat,
In a dance-off that makes everyone compete.
With hops and giggles, they bounce all around,
Until one spins out, tumbles down to the ground!

As stars twinkle down from their heavenly bars,
The nighttime creatures recount all the scars.
With laughter and moans, they bask in delight,
For tomorrow brings new tales in the light!

Dances in the Dappled Sunlight

In the warm sunshine, the fireflies twirl,
Chasing their shadows with a little swirl.
A bear in the thicket grows curious and bold,
Trips on a twig and tumbles uncontrolled!

The playful fox struts with a silly flair,
Wiggling his tail, without a single care.
But a splashing stream gives him quite a fright,
As he jumps back—oh, what an amusing sight!

The butterflies flutter, all colors and styles,
While flowers gossip with their blooming smiles.
A skipping snail moves at a leisurely pace,
But slips on a petal—oh what a race!

As day melts away and the sun says goodbye,
The critters recount their adventures up high.
A round of applause for the antics they bring,
In their whimsical world, where they dance and sing!

Echoing Dreams in the Green

In the woods where whispers play,
Squirrels dance in a comical way,
Trees chuckle as branches twist,
Nature's laughter, none can resist.

Bugs wear hats and prance around,
While rabbits hop without a sound,
They giggle at the mossy floor,
And plot mischief for days galore.

A chipmunk juggles acorns tall,
The wind joins in, almost a brawl,
Leaves rustle with vibrant glee,
As critters sip their herbal tea.

So come and join this merry scene,
Where laughter lives, and joy's routine,
In the heart of the vibrant glade,
Funny tales in sunlight played.

Tales of the Timeless Timber

Once a tree told a joke or two,
About a squirrel wearing a shoe,
It laughed so hard, it shook a limb,
Causing birds to sing off-key and grim.

The ants all gathered, ears perked wide,
To hear the punchlines, side by side,
Mice rolled on roots, their bellies ached,
As laughter echoed, the forest baked.

A wise old owl in glasses bright,
Tells punchlines deep into the night,
His feathered friends all hoot with cheer,
A nightly show that's held so dear.

With every trunk a story made,
The timber's tales will never fade,
In this green embrace, let joy ignite,
Where laughter dances with pure delight.

Sighs of the Majestic Cedars

Oh, the cedars stand so tall and proud,
But who knew they could giggle aloud?
With every breeze, they shake with joy,
   Their limbs wave like a merry toy.

A raccoon slipped on the morning dew,
The towering trees laughed, if they only knew,
   That even they could have a fall,
   As squirrels laughed, the best of all!

The shadows flickered with each bright whim,
   As barky jokes made the sunlight dim,
   And all the critters gathered 'round,
   To soak in laughter's gentle sound.

Underneath the grand green canopies,
   Life's funny moments float like leaves,
In this woodland wonder where hilarity thrives,
   Majestic cedars hold laughter's lives.

Legends Carved in Bark

On sturdy trunks, old tales reside,
Of naughty squirrels who never hide,
They say the roots can twist and shout,
When acorns fall and critters pout.

A mischievous fox once swiped a hat,
Left by a human, imagine that!
The trees all giggled at his sly spree,
As wind chimed in with a cheeky glee.

Moose tell stories of silly strife,
While bunnies munch on leafy life,
The legends carved in bark so grand,
Are filled with laughs across the land.

Nature's jester in patches bright,
Where chuckles carry throughout the night,
In every tree, a tale so keen,
The laughter lingers, evergreen.

Nature's Lullaby Beneath Starlit Pines

In the forest, a babbling brook,
Lulls the squirrels from their nook.
Raccoons bring their midnight snacks,
While owls are plotting their comical acts.

Beneath the stars, the critters dance,
As frogs take turns in a sing-and-prance.
The pine trees sway with a giggling breeze,
Nature's laughter floats with such ease.

Mice wear hats made of acorn caps,
While beetles organize tiny laps.
The moon winks down with a grin so wide,
In this woodland party, there's nowhere to hide.

So join the fun where shadows creep,
Where laughter hides and secrets leap.
Under pines, life's a playful jest,
Nature's lullaby, simply the best!

Reflections from the Woodland Water

By the pond, the frogs perform,
In costumes bright, their laughs transform.
Fish beneath wear painted scales,
While ducks write down their crazy tales.

A heron preens as it checks its hair,
While dragonflies buzz about in the air.
The reflections ripple with a grin,
As turtles join in, laughing within.

Bubbles rise with giggles from the deep,
As otters slide down a slippery leap.
The water's mirror, a stage so grand,
For woodland friends, in laughter they stand.

So dip your toes in this lively spree,
Where every splash brings glee and glee.
Nature's water, sparkling and bright,
Holds secrets of joy for every night!

Dreamscapes of the Greenery

In fields of green where the daisies sway,
Lying on the grass, dreaming all day.
A butterfly lands on a dandelion bed,
Causing the ants to dance with dread.

Trees wear crowns made of twinkling lights,
While crickets hold concerts of silly sights.
The breeze tells jokes that only it knows,
As all the flowers giggle in rows.

Bees in tuxedos buzz old school tunes,
As wind whispers jokes to the cheeky raccoons.
The earth wears a smile, so broad and wide,
In this dreamscape, hilarity won't hide.

So close your eyes, let laughter roam,
In the greenery, we all feel at home.
Nature's humor, a sweet surprise,
Lifts spirits high beneath the skies!

The Solace of Leafy Whispers

In every rustle, the leaves share a joke,
As squirrels bust out their best dance stoke.
Branches wave like hands in the air,
While chipmunks chuckle without a care.

Hide and seek in the lush, green maze,
Where sunlight flickers in its playful phase.
The canopy giggles with shadows that play,
Telling stories of mischief in a light-hearted way.

The woodland friends trade silly puns,
Every critter's caught in the laughter runs.
With twigs for wands, they cast silly spells,
Creating giggles that ringing bells.

So sit awhile, and soak in the cheer,
Where leafy whispers fill the atmosphere.
Nature's laughter, a balm for the soul,
Brings joy to the heart, makes the spirit whole!

Haunting Notes of the Hollow

In the hollow, a ghost plays jazz,
While owls clap and the raccoons razz.
A bat with a hat, dancing in flight,
Scratching its head at the curious sight.

The trees are swaying, tap dancing too,
A squirrel crowds in, finds his groove anew.
With acorns as drums, a nutty parade,
In this wild concert, the forest's unafraid.

Whispers of the Wind-Swept Pines

The pines are gossiping, oh what a tale,
Of a lost shoe and a goat with a veil.
They snicker and sway, keeping it light,
As the sun tickles branches, what a delight!

A breeze starts to chuckle, quickens the pace,
As a chipmunk in shades takes a sunbathing space.
'Twas a wild party last night,' he squeaks with a grin,
With the forest all buzzed on the nectar of gin!

Footfalls on the Leaf-Littered Path

Footfalls crunching, what a sound,
As critters join in, hopping around.
A parade of rascals, oh what a mess!
Leaves fly up high in a colorful dress!

A turtle tripped over a wayward shoe,
Cursed by the muck and the goo.
A rabbit did giggle, then rolled in the leaves,
Saying, 'There's always fun when the forest believes!'

Sounds of Serenity in the Forest

There's serenity mixed with a chortle or two,
As trees whisper secrets in the morning dew.
A squirrel in a cloak shares tales quite absurd,
Of a sloth who sets world records, unheard!

The brook hums a tune while frogs keep the beat,
As turtles squeeze in for a front-row seat.
A chorus of laughter from every green sprite,
Making peace in the woods feel decidedly light!

The Spirit of the Enchanted Woods

In the woods where the squirrels play,
The trees giggle in a quirky way.
Mushrooms wear hats, all cute and green,
They dance with the grass, a sight unseen.

The owls hoot jokes, they're quite the crowd,
Even the shy rabbits join, loud and proud.
A deer struts by, with swagger and flair,
Says, 'Who wore it better?' as he takes air!

Beneath the canopy, the branches sway,
A chorus of crickets join in the play.
With firefly lights, they start to rave,
Flashing 'disco' like they're little knaves.

So if you wander through this mindful maze,
Keep your ears open for laugh-filled days.
The spirit here is fun, bright, and spry,
In the woods where giggles and sunshine lie.

Rhapsody of the Emerald Hues

In fields of green where shadows gleam,
The flowers gossip and the grass does beam.
A butterfly wore her brightest dress,
Chasing a bee who just couldn't guess.

The trees tell tales of their past lives,
Of squirrels who once were the king of hives.
They share old secrets about the breeze,
Who tickles the branches and makes them tease.

With a splash of mud, the rabbits dive,
In games of tag, they truly thrive.
As bubbles float from a nearby brook,
They giggle so hard, you'd think it's a book!

In this vivid realm of laughter bright,
Every moment's a cheerful delight.
Each hue sings a song, wild and free,
In the symphony of nature's spree.

Silhouettes of Serenity in the Green

In the quiet glade where shadows sprout,
The mushrooms giggle, there's little doubt.
A squirrel rehearses his stand-up set,
While crickets cheer, they've placed their bet.

The tiny brook whispers secrets so sweet,
Even the stones have tapped their feet.
A fox in a scarf struts by with style,
He's got the charm to make you smile.

Each fern is a dancer, swaying low,
To tunes of the wind with a whimsical flow.
A raccoon juggles the acorns he's found,
While the laughter of trees echoes all around.

With every rustle and fluttering sound,
You'll find whimsy in this playful ground.
Where nature's humor and charm combine,
A merry adventure, a whimsical vine.

The Pulse of Nature's Heartbeat

Nature beats with a comical heart,
Where even the veggies play their part.
The carrots dance in their little patch,
While onions tease with a sly little snatch.

The sunflowers nod in rhythm and rhyme,
To tunes of the birds that chime in time.
A crow cracks jokes from an ancient oak,
Leaving the leaves in a fit of croak.

A hedgehog pops from a grassy abode,
Says, 'Join the fun, it's a laughter code!'
Every twig shakes with a chuckle or two,
As lilies giggle, and daisies boo-hoo.

In this garden of giggles, so bright and bold,
Nature's joy's a story that's always told.
So come and play where the wild things run,
In the heartbeat of nature, laughter's begun!

Footfalls in the Dappled Light

In the woods where shadows play,
Squirrels dance and jump all day.
I trip on roots that seem to grin,
Nature laughs with every spin.

A rabbit hides, then makes a leap,
While I'm tangled in a heap.
Every branch waves high and low,
Awkward me, just putting on a show.

The sun pokes through with golden beams,
I chase the light, or so it seems.
But with each turn, I find a wall—
Next time I'll just stick to the mall.

As leaves fall down like confetti cheer,
I dare not stand—oh, what a fear!
But then I smile, wide and bright,
Because nature's silly here tonight.

Chants from the Living Green

Amidst the trees, the whispers flow,
A tune sung soft by winds that blow.
But every note is off the beat,
I waltz with roots and trip on my feet.

A crow takes flight, then drops a snack,
I stare in awe, then hear a clack.
It's just my shoe that made the sound,
In this living green, I'm always bound.

Beneath the boughs, the squirrels chat,
"Look at that guy! It's quite a spat!"
With laughter ringing in the air,
I join the fun and lose my hair.

The rhythm grows with every step,
I shimmy, shake, then do inept.
With every clumsy leap I try,
The plants erupt in giggles nigh.

Whispers Through the Pines

A breeze floats by with secrets low,
Pines try to giggle, but I don't know.
I wave hello, get poked instead—
It seems these trees can be quite led.

With every turn, a branch whips round,
I duck and weave, but I hear a sound.
"Nice moves," they croon, "keep up the dance!"
Just hold my breath, and not a chance.

A fox trots by with style and grace,
I stumble over, what a race!
His laughing eyes say, "Try again!"
But limbs are tangled like my brain.

In playful air, the branches sway,
While all around, the critters play.
I join their fun, though I am sore,
Nature's knack for fooling I adore.

Reverberations of the Forest

The trees are tall, the sunlight's bright,
I trip over roots, try to take flight.
The forest chuckles with each fall,
A funny game for one and all.

With vines that twist and twirls that spin,
A dance with danger, let's begin!
I land in moss, that soft embrace,
Who knew that falling could be such grace?

The birds above respond with cheeps,
"Watch your step, or lose your keeps!"
But laughter rings in tranquil glades,
A merry cheer in leafy shades.

As twilight dims and shadows grow,
I wave goodbye, put on a show.
With every echo, crisp and clear,
I leave the woods, a bit more cheer.

Symphony of the Swaying Branches

The branches dance in playful cheer,
While squirrels sing, a concert near.
Leaves shake hands with the puffed-up breeze,
As birds rehearse their chirpy tease.

A rabbit grins, it's quite a show,
The deer clap hooves, they steal the show.
Frogs don tuxedos, croak along,
Nature's jesters in this merry throng.

The ants wear hats, parade in line,
While zippy bees bring honey wine.
A raccoon juggles acorns with flair,
The forest laughs, what a wild affair!

As twilight approaches, the giggles fade,
But nature's laughter will not evade.
Under the stars, they settle down,
Tomorrow's song will spin around.

Secrets Carried by the Breeze

A whisper floats through leafy sails,
As dandelions tell their tales.
The wind, a cheeky little sprite,
Spills morning gossip, oh what a sight!

Trees lean in with curious ears,
As chipmunks chatter without fears.
Every twig has its say, it seems,
Imagining life as wild as dreams.

A crow cracks jokes with witty grace,
While shadows dance in a playful race.
The breeze, a trickster, laughs aloud,
Turning every frown to a giggling crowd.

At sunset's close, the chatter shall wane,
But friendship lingers, like sweet champagne.
Tomorrow's breeze will blow anew,
With secrets fresh, and laughter too.

Cadence of the Hidden Glade

In a glade where the wild things play,
The flowers giggle, come what may.
A turtle waltzes, slow and grand,
While bunnies hop to an unseen band.

Froggies leap, a minuet fine,
They sip on dew and sip on twine.
The mushrooms pop with humor bright,
Holding court till the fall of night.

Hares in hats, what a curious sight,
Debate the stars, who's wrong or right.
In this merry nook, joy takes flight,
As crickets compose a symphony light.

When night descends, the laughing dims,
Yet stars twinkle in playful whims.
Tomorrow's tune shall be a delight,
Sweet echoes of joy, a pure delight.

Tones of the Twilight Woods

Twilight glimmers on laughter's face,
As shadows wiggle in a lively pace.
The owl hoots puns from high above,
While mice play hide and seek with love.

Chirping crickets, a band of cheer,
In every note, a chuckle near.
Fireflies flicker with a twinkling grin,
In this woodland dance, joy begins.

The foliage rustles, hey, what's that?
A sneaky fox with a playful pat.
He dips and dives through tall night's cloak,
Shoots a look, then crackles a joke.

As the stars twinkle, the forest unwinds,
With laughter woven through all its finds.
Tomorrow's tales will grace the leaves,
In the playful woods, where mirth believes.

The Pulse of the Hidden Thicket

In the thicket, a squirrel's leap,
A dance so clumsy, it makes me weep.
He gathers acorns, keeps them in stacks,
Yet forgets where he hid them, what a lax!

A rabbit hops with a coat of grey,
Wearing sneakers, runs in a funny way.
Chasing tails on old mossy logs,
While pondering deep, 'Am I a dog?'

The woodpecker taps a rhythmic beat,
To the tune of an old, rusty street.
While bees in hats sip nectar sweet,
Planning a heist; can't be discreet!

In this thicket, laughter prevails,
Where even the trees tell silly tales.
Each whisper and rustle, a joke unfolds,
Nature's mirth in green, uncontrolled!

Chasing the Soft Embrace of Shadows

A shadow slides, a lizard's race,
His tiny feet, a comic chase.
Beneath the sun, he makes a dash,
Wiggles that make me want to laugh!

A snail so slow, he's taking bets,
On who will win; it's all in jest.
The rabbit snickers as time drips by,
While the tortoise dreams of flying high.

The trees sway, sharing quirky lines,
Of dapper owls in funny designs.
Their branches sway with laughter anew,
As shadows embrace, in a whimsical hue.

In twilight glow, all come alive,
With chuckles shared, they twist and jive.
A world of shadows, where giggles thrive,
Nature's comedy, where all can dive!

Nature's Hidden Conversations

Leaves gossip lightly in the breeze,
Whispering tales of silly trees.
One claims he's taller, the other just sighs,
When a squirrel mocks from down low, oh my!

The toad croaks truths with a twist of rhyme,
Confusing the ants; they just can't climb.
A frog joins in with a lolloping grin,
'What's hopping now?' Oh, let the games begin!

Beneath the boughs where shadows play,
The crickets tell jokes at the end of the day.
While a wise old owl snoozes nearby,
Dreaming of who'll catch the biggest pie!

These hidden talks, a comedic scene,
In a world where nothing is ever routine.
Nature's laughter spills wide and free,
Turning each moment into glee!

The Call of the Wild Fern

A fern stands proud, with a feathered crown,
Claiming it's king of this leafy town.
The daisies giggle, their heads held high,
'Your reign is short-lived, oh, don't be shy!'

A caterpillar wobbles, dreaming of flight,
On a broccoli stalk, it feels oh so right.
'Next week,' it vows, 'I shall soar with flair,'
But for now, just munching—what a cute affair!

The wind whispers secrets, tickling the fronds,
While a playful stream tosses around its bonds.
Laughter erupts from the snappy old reeds,
As nature plays on, planting funny seeds.

In this wild space where antics thrive,
Each plant and critter is happily alive.
A symphony of chuckles, a green delight,
The call of the realm, a comical sight!

Sagas Beneath the Verdant Canopy

In the woods where squirrels plan,
A heist for acorns, oh what a scam!
A raccoon wears a mask, quite chic,
While talking trees giggle with a creak.

A bear in shades, he struts with flair,
Chasing butterflies, with little care.
A fox with socks takes dainty steps,
While owls hoot jokes and fill their reps.

Fungi in hats throw a funky dance,
As rabbits compete in a hopping prance.
The pines whisper tales of silly blunders,
As laughter rolls like occasional thunders.

So gather 'round this woodland jest,
Where nature's antics are at their best.
With each mischief, the forest sways,
In whimsical nights and sunny days.

Interlude in the Misty Boughs

In a fog, the mushrooms wear little coats,
Debating if they're squishy or just boats.
A sloth on a branch, he snores out loud,
While crickets hold a rave, feeling proud.

Tall trees gossip about the breeze,
Who tickles them softly, just to tease.
A chipmunk's dance is a sight to see,
Twisting and turning, wild and free.

The otters glide by in a splendid line,
Trading stories over mud pie wine.
The mist swirls round, a playful friend,
In this silly saga that will not end.

So join the fun, let laughter bloom,
In a place full of joy, and no hint of gloom.
The trees nod along as the day is done,
In the woods, dear friend, we all share the fun.

Voices from the Woodland Depths

Furry creatures with tales to tell,
From rabbits who thump to frogs that swell.
A hedgehog rolls like a tiny ball,
While crickets invent an up-tempo call.

Beneath the branches, the stories sprout,
Of a squirrel's mishap, oh, no doubt!
The acorns fall, a clumsy rain,
And laughter erupts; it's a wild refrain.

A deer in the glade pulls a funny face,
As a crow mocks him at a rapid pace.
The owls chuckle in hoots and peeps,
While whispers dance in the woodsy leaps.

With every rustle, a chuckle ignites,
Nature's comedy under moonlit nights.
So find your joy in the woodland beat,
And dance beneath the leafy seat.

Chronicles of the Rustling Underbrush

Down low in the brush, the stories swirl,
From silly tortoises who coil and twirl.
A fawn prances as it trips on a root,
While hedgehogs squeak in their prickly suit.

A mischievous fox steals a bee's grand prize,
With honey dripping all over his eyes.
The snakes crack jokes in their slithering way,
While shadows dance wildly at the end of the day.

A tapestry spun with laughter so bright,
In the heart of the woods, a delightful sight.
With every rustle, a giggle does rise,
From the smallest critters to the tall, wise guys.

So listen closely when the leaves are a-grin,
For each chuckle hides where the fun may begin.
Join in the ruckus, let your spirit run free,
In the rustling underbrush, where all laugh with glee.

The Voice of the Verdant Realm

In a forest full of trees, they chatter,
Squirrels rant and raves, oh what a clatter.
A squirrel stole my sandwich, can you believe?
His tiny hands wiggled, with tricks up his sleeve.

The owls hoot puns that make us snort,
While rabbits tell jokes of a very short sort.
The mushrooms giggle, they can't keep still,
Nature's comedy club, an unending thrill.

Deer dance awkwardly in silly formations,
Chasing each other with grand aspirations.
The brook sings loudly, but all it can say,
Is "You can't catch me, I'm flowing away!"

The trees shake branches, a rhythmic spree,
With swaying leaves that tickle my knee.
In this green realm where laughter's a seam,
Nature's a jester, the punchline supreme!

Songs Carried by the Wind

A breeze that's playful hums through the pines,
Tickling the leaves and cracking up vines.
"It's my turn to sing!" the gusty winds shout,
As I run with my hat, laughter's about!

The grass snaps back, like a rubbery friend,
Each blade a comedian that never will end.
The sky's in stitches, clouds puff up with glee,
"Why so serious? Let's float wild and free!"

Chirping crickets join in, with a beat oh so sly,
"Why did the chicken cross? To dance on the fly!"
Each note in the air is a smile in disguise,
Nature's chorus of giggles, no one defies.

The sun on my face feels like warmth-born cheer,
A parade of laughs that all creatures can hear.
The wind waves goodbye, with a wink as it glides,
"Don't forget to have fun, I'm always outside!"

Lullabies from the Deep Green

The treetops are giggling, whispering low,
As the fireflies wink to put on a show.
A baby bear yawns, with a sleepy stare,
"Who stole my honey? Where's my snack with care?"

The crickets compose sweet melodies fine,
While the owls recite tales of good bedtime wine.
A chorus of creatures, serenade the night,
"Sleep well, little one, all's cozy and right!"

The gentle breezes rock the limbs to and fro,
"Close your eyes, enjoy, let your dreams gently flow."
Bunny hopped by, with a pillow of clover,
"This lullaby won't stop until the day's over!"

With twinkling stars as the audience bright,
Nature croons softly, a warm-hearted sight.
So snuggle in tight; laughter's catching your z's,
The green's lullabies bring the sweetest of dreams!

Memories Wrapped in Moss

In the woodland where laughter is softly embraced,
Old logs tell tales with a humorous taste.
"Remember the day when the rain took a trip?
We slipped and we slid, oh what a wild trip!"

Moss rugs lay waiting, for naps and for spins,
Each patch a reminder of all of our wins.
A frog cracked a joke, made us jump from our feet,
"Life's a big splash! Try the puddles for treats!"

The trees have grown old, but their jokes stay aglow,
"Why did the crow sit on the telephone pole?"
They chuckle in time, as the sunlight does gleam,
Nature's own sitcom, a whimsical dream.

Lullabies from the Deep Green

The treetops are giggling, whispering low,
As the fireflies wink to put on a show.
A baby bear yawns, with a sleepy stare,
"Who stole my honey? Where's my snack with care?"

The crickets compose sweet melodies fine,
While the owls recite tales of good bedtime wine.
A chorus of creatures, serenade the night,
"Sleep well, little one, all's cozy and right!"

The gentle breezes rock the limbs to and fro,
"Close your eyes, enjoy, let your dreams gently flow."
Bunny hopped by, with a pillow of clover,
"This lullaby won't stop until the day's over!"

With twinkling stars as the audience bright,
Nature croons softly, a warm-hearted sight.
So snuggle in tight; laughter's catching your z's,
The green's lullabies bring the sweetest of dreams!

Murmurs Beneath the Canopy

In the woods, a squirrel leaps,
Chasing dreams or acorn heaps.
Laughter echoes from the boughs,
As wind complains, "What's this, now?"

A bear wearing shoes, what a sight,
Dancing clumsily, try as it might.
Trees giggle softly with their creaks,
Nature's humor seldom speaks.

A frog croaks jokes to a passing deer,
"Why so serious? Let's find some cheer!"
With every rustle, whispers abound,
In this jolly green world, joy is found.

Reflections of Light through Leaves

Sunbeams tickle the forest floor,
As a snail races—oh, what a chore!
"Look at me!" the tiny critter yells,
Faster than a turtle, in its proud swells.

Beneath the beams, a wise old owl,
Snoozes loudly, while the others scowl.
"Wake up, wise one, the day's at hand!"
But snores erupt like a marching band.

A butterfly spins, chasing its tail,
Laughing at shadows that flail and flail.
"Catch me if you can!" it flutters by,
While a slug rolls its eyes, giving a sigh.

Secrets of the Timeless Grove

There's a secret club beneath the pine,
Mice tell tales over a glass of brine.
The raccoon's wearing a top hat neat,
"Last meeting's snacks? Oh, what a treat!"

Old tree stumps gather for their chat,
Discussing life, and where they're at.
"Remember the time we got chopped down?"
"No way, man! We deserved that crown!"

Roots intertwine, a dance so fine,
While beetles compose a wacky line.
"Let's shimmy to the river's roll!"
All join in, forgetting control.

A Symphony of Nature's Breath

A rustle here, a shuffle there,
In this realm, what a wild fare!
Crickets play a concert's delight,
While frogs join in, a hilarious sight!

Leaves sway gently, a rhythmic beat,
As squirrels perform a tap-dance feat.
"Encore, encore!" the crowd shouts loud,
Admiring moves, they're feeling proud.

The grand orchestra is quite bizarre,
With buzzing bees and a loud guitar.
So sit back, relax, and let it unfold,
Nature's gig is pure comedy gold!

Harmony Beneath the Forest Roof

Squirrels chatter in a great debate,
Who buried the acorns? They can't relate.
A raccoon laughs, a fox rolls his eyes,
In this leafy theater, oh what a surprise!

The owls hoot wisdom, or so they claim,
While the woodpeckers drum, creating a game.
The rabbits all hop, as they share their dreams,
Of carrots so big, or so it seems!

Down by the creek, the frogs start to sing,
Making a ruckus, like it's a fling.
A dance of the critters, in feathers and fur,
In this sunlit grove, there's no time to stir!

As twilight descends, the antics still thrive,
The night critters giggle, feeling quite alive.
With fireflies buzzing, the party's not done,
In this forest club, everyone has fun!

Elysian Serenades of the Thicket

Beneath the tall pines, a concert did break,
All creatures assembled, for goodness sake!
The badgers were drumming, the owls kept time,
And the rabbits hopped by, in sync with the rhyme.

A fox tried to dance, and tripped on a leaf,
While the deer snorted laughter, in sheer disbelief.
They sang all night, till the stars took a peek,
Oh, what a sight, this woodland mystique!

The raccoons were juggling, acorns and nuts,
While the turtles cheered on, saying "What's up, guts?"
In this thicket of joy, every creature partakes,
With harmony blending, as the party awakes!

As dawn breaks the spell, the band must adjourn,
But not without promises of the next turn.
The trees whisper whispers, they'll keep the score,
For next time, oh yes, there'll be even more!

Lament of the Lonesome Tree

Once stood a tree, oh so tall and so grand,
Who dreamed of some friends, oh in this land.
But the critters all laughed, and said with a grin,
"We're busy right now, come join in our din!"

"I hear you," said tree, "but I'm rooted right here,
And I have no legs, my dear, have no fear!"
But the rabbits just hopped, the squirrels just ran,
While the old tree sighed, "I wish I had a plan."

Then one day a bird, perched high on a branch,
Said, "Let's have some fun, come on, take a chance!"
So they threw a big party, a spring fling at best,
With leaves wearing hats, oh what a jest!

Now the tree isn't lonesome, he's part of the crew,
With critters and whispers, beneath skies so blue.
And he chuckles at tales of his days spent alone,
For friendships can bloom anywhere, even stone!

Echoes of the Wild Willows

Down by the river, where the willows sway,
A bunch of young ducks had wandered to play.
They quacked out a rhythm, a tune nice and sweet,
As the frogs stomped along, tapping webbed feet.

The fish in the current all wiggled with glee,
While the old turtle grumbled, "Just let it be!"
But the willows kept swaying, with fabric so green,
Creating a dance floor, as all joined the scene.

A raccoon swung by, with a hat tipped just so,
"What's this shindig about? I'd love to know!"
With a wink and a nudge, he joined in the fun,
For laughter is best when shared with everyone.

As the sun dipped low, the party still roared,
With tales of the day, and food they adored.
Under willows so wild, the critters were free,
In this riverside jamboree, all danced with glee!

Melodies of the Sylvan Shadows

In a glen, the squirrels dance,
With acorns flying every chance.
A rabbit hops like it's on beat,
While a frog joins in with tiny feet.

The trees sway 'neath a silly tune,
As raccoons croon to the silver moon.
A woodpecker pecks in time, oh dear,
Out of rhythm, but who would care?

The owls hoot with a mocking cheer,
Calling out to the happy deer.
Each twig snaps like a comical joke,
While laughter stirs in the old oak smoke.

Together they create a song,
In the forest where all belong.
With giggles shared amongst the leaves,
The woodland revels, no one believes!

Hushed Conversations Among the Branches

The pine whispers secrets with a grin,
While the birch giggles, letting fun begin.
Leaves rustle like a group in chat,
"Did you see that bird? It fell flat!"

The willow shakes its leafy head,
"Sounds like someone tripped on their thread!"
Branches chuckle at the squirrel's plight,
Chasing its tail, oh what a sight!

"Did the fox really think he could sneak?"
As pinecones plop, and laughter peaks.
Echoes of mirth reverberate through,
A squirrel's misstep, and off they flew!

So hush, listen close to the laughter,
In every leaf, there's joy to capture.
For the trees share tales, both funny and wise,
In conversations where humor never dies.

Serenade of the Ancient Woods

Within the grove a melody strays,
Where the critters engage in playful displays.
A bear does ballet, oh what a sight!
While the badger conducts; he's quite polite.

The hedgehogs hum an off-key song,
As the porcupines cheer, "You can't go wrong!"
The toads tap dance, in their own peculiar way,
And party under a moonlit ray.

"Watch the fawn spin, so fresh and spry!"
Squeals the crow perched on high in the sky.
The roots thrum like drums in a trance,
As the plants sway to this whimsy dance.

Old trees grumble about youth today,
Yet even they can't resist the sway.
Each bark has a snicker, each leaf a chuckle,
In the ancient woods, it's always a cuddle.

The Call of the Greenheart

In the heart of the woods, a whisper stirs,
Where the bushes gossip, and the grass purrs.
The sunbeams tickle the mossy ground,
As nature plays symphonies all around.

"Why did the tree go to the party?"
"Because it didn't want to be too hearty!"
The ferns giggle, their fronds a-waving,
At critters with moves that are quite misbehaving.

"Be careful, the wind's in a playful mood!"
It teases the branches, oh how rude!
Nestled in shadows, laughter takes flight,
Gaining momentum, through day and night.

So join the fun where the green things grow,
Every leaf and twig shares a little show.
In this merry realm of mischief and mirth,
All creatures unite, to celebrate their birth!

www.ingramcontent.com/pod-product-compliance
Lightning Source LLC
Chambersburg PA
CBHW071823160426
43209CB00003B/184